MW00764134

The Magic of Points

The greatest way to travel

F. G. McCulley, Jr.

My Perspectivetoo Publishing
New York, NY

Cover and book design by

F. G. McCulley, Jr.

Illustrations by: Joseph Matose,

Award Winning Artist

Front cover photo: Castaway Cay, Bahamas

Back cover photo: Capri, Italy

First printing, September 2015

ISBN: 978-1517274146

For more information, please visit

www.myperspectivetoo.com

DEDICATION

This book is dedicated in memory of my sister, Lisa A. Silvia and my dad, Frank G. McCulley, Sr., for giving me the courage to follow my passion.

Introduction

The Magic Of points

The greatest way to travel

- If you have dreams of travel and think you can't afford it this book is for you.

- This book is about how to earn points and how to use them.

- You can turn points into money.

- This book is not just about travel it's what you can do with points.

- Learn the 5 easy steps to earn thousands of points.

- Take the first step in acquiring this knowledge to save you or make you thousands of dollars.

- You don't have to fly to earn points or use them for flights.

Introduction (Cont'd)

- This is a step by step guide on how to earn and travel on points and how to redeem them.

- This is the method I have used to travel all over and save me thousands.

- Redeem points for car rentals, hotels, cruises, gift cards and more.

- You will be amazed how fast and easy it is to earn points.

****

I am in no way affiliated with Southwest Airlines or their Partners or any companies mentioned in this book. The statements are my own personal opinions and based on my own experiences.

TABLE OF CONTENTS

ACKNOWLEDGMENTS

I want to thank all my family and friends for their support and a special thank you to my wife.

Chapter 1

Let me start out by saying I love to travel and want to do it as much as possible, but as we all know it can be very expensive! I found out how to earn and use points to travel.

My wife and I travel all over from one to two night stays, long weekends, or weeks at a time. Our friends and family think we have hit the lottery because we travel so much and go on so many vacations!

I found ways to earn points by just making a few changes in my life and in doing so I have been greatly rewarded and it's all thanks to Southwest Airlines Rapid Rewards. Southwest Airlines may not service your immediate area or you may not even fly on Southwest and that's ok. This is a book on how to earn points and what they can be redeemed for.

Over the past 6 years I have earned enough points so that when I fly I don't pay for my tickets, I use points. Southwest Airlines has a great perk called the Companion Fare.

Anyone who earns 110,000 points in one calendar year can have someone fly with them for free every time they fly for one full year with no limits. I have earned this perk six years in a row and have earned over 700,000 points. Over that time my wife has flown on the companion fare over 50 round trip flights for free! (Government fees apply $11.20) That was a savings of over $15,000!

For this reason I believe Southwest Airlines Rapid Rewards program is the best. What other company would let you take your companion for free every time you fly for one full year for just earning 110,000 points in one year?

Southwest Airlines uses a points system and the points you earn don't expire and are very easy to redeem. You can use the points for almost everything including flights where ever Southwest Airlines fly's and there are no seat restrictions or blackout dates. You can use points for cruises, hotels, car rentals, international flights, event tickets, gift cards, other travel, and so much more and points are very easy to redeem. Let me explain what points are. Points are like imaginary money that you turn into real things. I want to make something very clear you don't need to fly to earn points. You can earn points many other ways and I will explain.

Points can also be redeemed for many things including gift cards and to me that is the same as cash. You are not limited to just using points for airline tickets. It only takes 3,000 points to get $25.00 gift cards or 5,000 points for $50.00 gift cards for places like Hard Rock Cafe, Footlocker, iTunes, Lowe's, TJ Maxx, Alamo, Royal Caribbean, Carnival Cruise Lines, Walmart, Omaha Steaks, Target and many more. So let's start earning points... It's all about points!

Before we get started, I want to tell you all the ways I earn and use points so you will have a better understanding of what I'm about to tell you. I will show you exactly what you need to do to start earning thousands and thousands points so that you can be successful and take the vacations of your dreams or just earn some extra money.

It all began with opening up a free Southwest Airlines Rapid Reward account. This account is like a bank and its where all the points I will be earning will go and I will know how I earned them.

With this account set up I realized that whenever I needed to make a purchase for anything it was best to charge it to my credit card rather than pay cash because I would earn points. So now I charge everything even if it costs a dollar and I pay my credit card bill in full every month as to not pay any interest. The only credit card I use is the Chase Southwest Airlines credit card. They offer me 1 point for every dollar I spend and 2 points for every dollar I spend with Southwest Partners. (The Partners are listed on page 47 or on Southwest Airlines website).

I also have two Southwest Airlines credit cards in my name, one for me, one for my wife and one card for my mother-in-law. I have my mother-in-law charge everything she needs and she pays me at the end of the month. All the points earned go into my Rapid Rewards account each month.

Again, I charge everything I can and don't use cash at all! I will pay all my bills like electric, phone, etc., that I can on my credit card as long as I'm not charged a fee for it because I now know purchases equal points and points add up so fast It's amazing!!!!

I have two Southwest Airlines credit cards although it's not necessary to have one but it's a great way to earn extra points. I received 50,000 points when I got mine. That was a great head start on earning points.

I'm always looking on the Southwest Airlines website for ways to earn extra points. I also look on the Southwest Rapid Rewards Shopping website which is where I can shop online stores to earn extra points and also check the Southwest Rapid Rewards Dining website which is where I can earn extra points for dining at participating restaurants and bars. These websites offer many ways to earn bonus points throughout the year and I definitely want to take advantage of that.

When I go out to dinner with friends and family and it's time to pay the bill they may want to pay the bill in cash. I will take all the cash and I will charge it on my credit card, pay the bill at the end of the month and collect all the points. I have also asked friends and family needing to make a big purchase to let me charge what they need and they would write me a check for it. That way I benefit from the points.

And when I travel and need to rent a car or stay in a hotel I always rent the car or hotel through Southwest Airlines website because they always have promotions and I can earn double or triple credits for booking directly through them and all the points earned will automatically go into my Rapid Reward account.

During the year, Southwest Airlines and their Partners have many promotions that I take advantage of like double points for flying into certain cities, or receive 5,000 points for referring someone to get the Rapid Reward credit card or 500 points for referring someone to get a Southwest Rapid Reward account. Another good one was when they offered a Marriott gift card.

I was able to purchase a $100.00-$500.00 gift card and received 6,000-12,000 points for doing that. The card has no expiration date and can be used at any Marriott for food or accommodations. Another great way I accumulate points is I sign up for all car rental and hotel reward programs which are free and link them to my Southwest account so that every time I use one of these Partners all the points go into my Rapid Rewards account automatically.

When you belong to these programs you receive so many free perks. One of the best is not waiting in long lines at the car rental counter I go right to the front of the line. At hotels I get free internet, sometimes a courtesy late check out, and so much more... and best of all the points!

The Southwest Airlines Rapid Reward Shopping website is where the majority of my points come from. This is where I earn extra points just for shopping on line with major realtors. There are hundreds and hundreds of stores. Each store lists the points you will get for shopping with them.

Let me give you an example, I needed something from Home Depot and it cost $300.00 I would not go to the store to purchase it. I would go to the Southwest Shopping website and find Home Depot listed as receiving 2 points extra points for every dollar spent. I would then be sent to the Home Depot website. I place my order and then pick it up at the store.

This means I will get 600 points for doing that (2 X $300.00). Then, because I used my Southwest credit card to make the purchase I got another 300 points. So with that one purchase I earned 900 points and that amount will be added to my Rapid Rewards account! Most people would pay in cash or debit and receive no points at all! So this is just one example of why I don't do that.

There have been many instances when Home Depot has offered up to 6 points for every dollar spent. I have earned so many points this way and all stores offer even more points from time to time.

I wanted to get a gift for my wife so I went to Southwest Airlines Rapid Rewards shopping website and found that they were offering gifts card for 15 points per dollar spent at magazineline.com. I purchased a $100.00 gift card (15 X $100.00) and earned 1,500 points for doing that. Then, I use that gift card at magazineline.com through the Southwest shopping site and they were offering 15 points for every dollar spent (15 X $100.00).

I used the gift card I just purchased and got another 1,500 points I only spent $100.00 but earned 3,000 points plus 100 points for a total (3,100 point) because I charged the original $100 on my credit card. Now do you see the power of points? I always want to see what gift cards they are offering because that is just extra points for free and you can do this over and over again.

I also like going out for dinner so I joined the Rapid Reward Dining Program which is where the merchant rewards you with points when you dine with them and all I had to do is register my credit card at Rapid Reward Dining. Now when I charge my bill at any participating restaurants and night clubs I will be earning points.

I receive 3 points for every dollar spent on dining, and an extra 10 points for every online review I complete! And again, all I had to do was register my credit card at Rapid Reward Dining. That was it, more free points!!!!

I also do free on-line surveys at E-rewards which is an Opinion Panel that is the world's leading online market research panel. As part of this exclusive panel, members have the opportunity to share their experiences with global brands about the products and services they offer.

In return for their time and opinions, members collect e-Rewards Currency for each study they complete, which can then be redeemed for a variety of rewards but I redeem them for Southwest Rapid Reward points. It's free and I average about 1,000-2,400 points per month.

I also do free on-line surveys at e-Miles it's an exclusive online program that rewards you for your time with airline miles, sponsor points, gift cards or other exciting reward options. It's absolutely free! As a member of e-Miles, you can earn free miles in just a few minutes a day simply by reading and responding to marketing messages based on my preferences.

I have just explained to you the ways that I earn points and know without a doubt that you will be as successful or even more successful than me at earning thousands and thousands of points. Now let's get you started earning points and once your set up it takes little or no effort to start earning points.

Chapter 2

Getting started

Step 1

Set up your free Southwest Airlines Rapid Reward account on the Southwest Airlines website. Just click on Join Rapid Rewards at the bottom of the page. Once you do you will be given a Rapid Reward number and free points for joining. This account is where all your earned points will go and you will know who you earned them from.

Helpful Tips

You can earn extra points throughout the year if you tell friends & family about Rapid Rewards and they open up an account.

Step 2

Apply for a Southwest Airlines Rapid Reward credit card on the Southwest Airlines website. You don't need to have this card but is recommended for all the potential points as I described.

Having this credit card is one part. You will be earning points for everything you charge to it and it adds up quick. You are spending the money anyway so why not take advantage of it! All Southwest partner purchases are doubled and all other purchases are dollar for dollar.

There is a fee for this card but for what you are getting is well worth it.

You will start out with 25,000 points (one time) when you charge $1,000.00 in the first three months and on your anniversary every year you will get another 3,000-6,000 points depending on which credit card you get.

Remember, 5,000 points can be redeemed for a $50.00 gift card so they are giving you back $50.00 every year.

Please don't worry that the card has an annual fee $69.00-$99.00. The benefits you receive by having the card is well worth the yearly fee! Just try to be smart and pay the balance in full every month to avoid interest charges! Remember my 700,000 points I earned in six years would have been $7,000.00 in gift cards but I redeemed mine for free flights.

Let me ask you, would you rather pay $294.00 for a round trip ticket or use 16,200 points of the 25,000 points they are giving you just for getting the card? Having the card is well worth the $69.00 or $99.00 annual fee.

Helpful Tips

You may know someone that has the Chase Southwest Rapid Rewards credit card and if they were to refer you for the card they may get 5,000 bonus points.

Remember all Partners charges are 2 points per dollar. You will receive notices to earn bonus points through the year.

Annual fee is $69.00-$99.00 but every year you get 3,000-6,000 anniversary points which you can redeem for $25.00 or $50.00 gift cards.

Best of all the 25,000 points you start with can redeem for $250.00 in gift cards. What a great deal!!!!!!!!

You can redeem points for gift cards for places like Hard Rock Cafe, Footlocker, iTunes, Lowes, TJ Maxx, Marshalls, Home goods, Alamo, Royal Caribbean, Carnival Cruise Lines, Walmart, Omaha Steaks, Target and many more.

You will also receive points for balance transfers from other credit cards. It is unbelievable how many ways there are to earn points.

If you're a business owner you should be charging everything you can to this card and also checking the Southwest Rapid Reward Shopping site for companies that you may be purchasing from to take advantage of the extra points.

Step 3

Go to Southwest Rapid Reward Dining website and sign up and register any credit card and provide your Rapid Reward number. You love to dine out and you may do it several times a week so why not earn points every time. As a member of Rapid Rewards Dining, you can earn extra points for going to your choice of thousands of participating restaurants, bars and clubs including many of your favorites!

Helpful Tips

When you go out with friends and family make sure you charge the bill on your new Southwest Airlines credit card to earn the points.

The best part is that you do not have to know if the bar or restaurant is participating in the dining program because you registered your credit card so the points would be earned automatically with no thought whatsoever. You can also earn bonus points for any reviews you do.

There are over 11,000 participating bars and restaurants throughout the USA.

Step 4

This one you do not have to join. Go to Rapid Rewards Shopping and log in with you Rapid Reward number to find participating on-line retailers, offers or products. You will receive points just for shopping!

You can shop online by category for things such as apparel, accessories, beauty and health, books, music, movies, computers electronics, department stores, entertainment, flowers, food and gifts, home gardening, auto, office, school, services, sports and recreation, and travel.

Helpful tips

You can earn from 1 point per dollar spent to 20 points per dollar spent or more with every store.

The best tip I can give you is to think about every purchase you need to make and think if there is a way to earn points doing it. Always check the Southwest Rapid Reward Shopping site to see if any stores are listed before you make a purchase.

I make so many purchases this way and earn thousands of extra points. All I have to do is shop for it on-line and have it delivered or pick it up at the store.

Examples:

I will go to the Southwest Airlines Rapid Rewards shopping website and be sent to the Walmart website. I will be given an extra point for everything I purchase so I'll purchase items like shaving cream, soap, shampoo, paper towels, anything I can think of. If I spend a hundred dollars I would get 100 points for making the purchase and another 100 points for charging it on my Rapid Reward credit card. Best of all, the items will be shipped to me or I go to the store to pick them up.

I needed to purchase new appliances and found on the Rapid Rewards shopping site that Sears was offering 4 points per dollar spent. I spent $1,800.00 and I received 7,200 points from that ($1,800.00 X 4) and $1,800.00 points from the credit card for a total of 9,000 points. Do you now see how fast they can add up?

Step 5

List of three survey companies:

e-miles

Sign up for on-line surveys at e-miles (IT'S FREE!)
Just go to e-miles website to enroll

Below - points redemption chart:

e-miles currency level 500 miles redeems for 500
Rapid Reward points

e-miles currency level 1,000 miles redeems for

1,000 Rapid Reward points

e-miles currency level 1,500 miles redeems for
1,500 Rapid Reward points

e-miles currency level 2,000 miles redeems for 2,000 Rapid Reward points

e-miles currency level 3,000 miles redeems for 3,000 Rapid Reward points

Valued opinions

Go to the Valued Opinions website.

As a Rapid Rewards member you can earn points by completing surveys through Valued Opinions.

Once a member of Valued Opinions, you will be sent market research surveys tailored to your interests for every survey you complete.

You will earn $0.50 and $5.00. The more surveys you take, the more rewards you will collect in no time at all.

You could have accumulated enough rewards to exchange for Rapid Rewards Points. Visit Southwest Airlines website Partner Promotions.

E-rewards

You will be given the opportunity to join through e-mail. If you are already a member of E-rewards below is a point redemption chart.

e-rewards currency level $15.00 redeem for 300 Rapid Reward points.

e-rewards currency level $25.00 redeem for 600 Rapid Reward points.

e-rewards currency level $50.00 redeem for 1,200 Rapid Reward points.

e-rewards currency level $100.00 redeem for 2,400 Rapid Reward points.

Helpful Tips

The offers for surveys come directly to your e-mail
so you don't have to think about them. And they
only take about 5-15 minutes to do them and they
are free.

Chapter 3

- **What you can do with points**

- **Ways to earn points and get double and triple points... for things you purchase!**

What you can do with points

All found on Southwest Airlines website. Fly on Southwest Airlines with no seat restrictions or blackout dates.

Fly on International flights, hotel stays at over 70,000 hotels worldwide, rent a car at various car rental companies like Alamo, Avis, Hertz, Dollar, National, and many more. You can also purchase gift cards with a variety of popular brands like Starbuck's, Walmart, iTunes, and many more.

Also Experiential Rewards including cruises, spa packages golf trips, MLB games, NFL games, concerts, etc.

From the Southwest Airlines home page click on Rapid Rewards then click on More Rewards. Now you are on the More Rewards homepage and this is where you can redeem your points for a wide variety of things including the items mentioned above.

Ways to earn points and get double and triple points... for things you purchase!

Log in to your Rapid Rewards account when booking air, hotel or car reservations because you get extra points if there is a promotion.

When you are about to make an online purchase always remember to check the Southwest Rewards shopping website to see if your store is listed and go to the site from there.

When making a purchase for everyday items always use your Southwest Rapid Reward credit card to make that purchase.

Do your free online surveys and redeem for points that you can transfer to your Southwest Rapid Reward account.

When you purchase a ticket and fly on Southwest you will receive 6 points per dollar spent for a Wanna Get Away ticket 10 points per dollar spent for a Anytime ticket and 12 points per dollar spent for a Business Select ticket.

When you dine at any of the participating restaurants and bars at Southwest Rapid Rewards Dining your earned points will be automatic because you linked to your credit card and gave your Rapid Reward number when you signed up.

Helpful Tips

When you pay for a Southwest Airlines Wanna Get Away ticket and don't use points you will get six times the price in points for the ticket ($300.00 ticket X 6) 1,800 points.

When you fly that flight and you will get another 600 points from the credit card ($300.00 X 2). Remember 2 points with Partners.

During the year Southwest and their Partners have promotions that you can take advantage of like double points for flying into a certain cities, purchasing a Marriott gift cards or signing up for a Hilton Honors credit card and getting 5,000 points and many others.

Southwest Airlines Partners- 2 points per dollar spent at:

Best Western	Alamo	Laquinta
Carlson Hotels	Avis	E-rewards
Choice Hotels	Budget	e-miles
Hyatt	Dollar	Mlife
Spg	Hertz	ScoreBig
Marriott	National	
Valued Opinions	payless	
Rocket Miles	Thrifty	
Super shuttle	Energy Plus	
Score Big	Everything Energy	
1-800flowers.com	Rapid Reward Shopping	
Reliant	Rapid Reward Dining	

Chapter 4

How to book the companion fare

If you are fortunate enough to earn 110,000 points in one calendar year you will receive the Companion Fare for one year. You will be given the opportunity to designate someone as the person you want to fly with you every time you fly.

Now you're ready to book a flight go to the Southwest Airlines website, log into your account, and book a flight for yourself. When you are done, that flight will now be in your account as upcoming flights. When you go to view that flight you will see where it says add companion and follow the steps and receive your companions confirmation number.

Helpful Tip

When booking a companion fare you are given two separate confirmation numbers... one for you and one for your companion. Keep in mind that you will both have to check in for the flight. You can also change the person you have designated as your companion three times.

When you need to cancel any ticket you purchased with points you will get all your points back.

How to fly free

Only use your points for flights and you will never have to pay for flights again. Try your best to earn the companion fare. This perk is so unbelievable to have.

(Government fees apply $11.20)

Helpful Tip

If you really want to try for the companion fare apply for the Southwest Airlines Rapid Rewards credit card as close to the beginning of the year as possible because the points you're going to get count down towards the companion fare. 110,000 points are needed for the companion fare.

You are going to get either 25,000 or 50,000 points for getting the credit card, so you are only going to need 60,000 or 85,000 more points for the rest of the year to earn it.

I want to use the least amount of points when booking a ticket so I like to book the ticket as early as I can. The prices of flights are sometimes cheaper when they first come out. To find out when the new flight schedule opens up go to Southwest Airlines website and click on flights/hotel/car then click on Flight Schedules. Flights are also cheaper on Tuesday's when Southwest comes out with their specials. Even if that's not the case, book a ticket when you see it because it always costs you more if the price goes up and you can always get your money or points back when the price goes down.

Chapter 5

- **How to save on Cruises**

- **How to book an airline ticket with points**

In my experience, I seldom book with cruise lines directly. I find that you get more perks when you book with companies like Cruise.com. You can get things like guest sail free, specialty dining packages, ultimate beverage packages, prepaid gratuities, internet packages, soda packages, onboard credits, reduction in deposits, and one night pre or post cruise hotel for free.

Helpful Tips

When you book any type of vacation whether it be a cruise, hotel, car rental, etc., always check to see if the price has gone down and if it has you can rebook it for free

Or, just cancel it and book it again. I do this all the time to save money!

When booking 7-14 night Caribbean cruises I would recommend flying to Puerto Rico and getting on the cruise from here. When taking a cruise that leaves from Puerto Rico you are stopping at more ports and you have less days at sea. Also, cruises are sometimes cheaper from Puerto Rico than the USA and the flights are sometimes cheaper.

How to book an airline ticket with points

The first thing you should do is go to the Southwest Airlines website and log into your Rapid Reward account. Then, you will fill out the flight information on where you want to go.

The next screen that you see you are going to be giving a choice of seeing the fares in cash or points and you want to choose points. On this screen, you should see the points for each flight. You can buy a one-way ticket or a round-trip ticket as long as you have the points in your account you can get that ticket. Next, follow the steps and you will have used your points for the ticket and receive your confirmation number.

Helpful Tips

Another way I save on flights that I purchase or book with points is to check to see if the fare has gone down in price or in points. I do this right up to the departure date of the flight. I log into my account and check to see what the price of the flight is then.

If the flight price or points have gone down I click on where it says change flight, make the change for free and the points go back into my account or I will get a credit to use the on a future flights.

You can also use your points to give someone else a free flight. Log into your account provide flight information, select show price in points, then where it says your name fill in the travelers name that the ticket is for.

When you need to cancel any ticket you purchased with points you get all you points back.

Chapter 6

- How to save when booking hotels

- How to save when booking car rentals

- How to earn even more points on car rentals

How to save when booking hotels

Southwest offers bonus points when booking through their website and you will also receive points if it's one of the partner brands

Helpful Tip

Join all of the hotel loyalty programs you can as to take advantage of all the perks that they may have to offer.

From the Southwest Airlines home page click on Special Offers and here you will find all hotel limited time offers and extra points.

How to save when booking car rentals

Car rentals rates are like the stock market, the prices change every day so book in advance and check the price even up to the day before the rental. You will be surprised to see that the price may have gone down.

Helpful tip

Join all of the car rental loyalty programs you can as to take advantage of all the perks that they may have to offer and you will not have to waste time standing in line.

Most rental car companies have self-service kiosk that also save time.

How to earn even more points on car rentals

From the Southwest Airlines home page click on Special Offers and here you will find all rental car extra point offers.

Chapter 7

Redeeming points

Ok, let's say you have some extra points you want to use and turn into money. What you would do is go to the Southwest Airlines website, click on Rapid Rewards and then click on More Rewards, and you will be brought to the Southwest Rapid Rewards More Rewards page and here you will be given the opportunity to shop with your points.

Once you are there, click on Gift Cards and you will be shown all the different gift cards you can get with your points.

This is where you can redeem your points. A $25.00 gift card redeems for 3,000 points and a $50 gift card would be 5,000 points.

So when I told you I had earned over 700,000 in six years I could have redeemed them for $7,000.00 in gift cards. It's so easy to do and no fees!

When you are redeeming points you have many choices to choose from like department stores, entertainment, restaurants, shopping, home office, resorts, golf experiences and many more.

You can get gift cards for places like Hard Rock, Footlocker, iTunes, Lowe's, TJ Maxx, Marshalls, Alamo, Royal Caribbean, Carnival Cruise Lines, Walmart, Omaha Steaks, Target and many more.

Helpful tip

When you want to get a gift for someone or shop for Christmas presents, remember you have all those free points that you can always use.

Just visit Southwest Rapid Rewards More Rewards website.

****

Now that you know how to earn and use points and whether you use them for travel or other things, I hope this knowledge brings you much success, memories, and to places you have always dreamed of.

ABOUT THE AUTHOR
F. G. McCulley, Jr.

I was an electrician for almost 20 years and although I was very good at it, I always felt like I should be doing something else. Losing people that are close to you makes you realize that there may not be a tomorrow and all the thoughts and things that you were going to do in the future may not happen.

All along I had been living with the thought "I can do it tomorrow" but now I do it today. I'm following my dreams and living life today. I've always had a passion for travel and have wanted to share that passion, and what better way than to write this book!